Dedicated to every sibling who loves someone born with a CHD.

In Memory of Liam, the boy whose life inspired these stories.

A Note to the Parents & Family

"Doctors Help Baby" is the first book in a series designed to assist parents and family walk your child(ren) through a younger sibling's hospital stay for a Congenital Heart Defect (CHD). Having to watch your new baby go through open heart surgery so young is very difficult for parents to experience. It can be even harder when you have other children. Even though they may be little, they have so many questions and fears, just like you. There are no right or wrong ways to feel as your family walks along side your Heart Warrior through open-heart surgery and the healing journey.

This book is designed to help you navigate the hospital experience with your older children so they can better understand what is happening to their newest sibling and process their emotions. As you share this book with your child about their sibling's specific situation. Encourage them to share how they are feeling about their sibling and all the changes that have occurred within your family.

Other resources can be found at: www.littlehearts.org, www.mendedhearts.org, and www.pted.org

You can also find local CHD support groups in an area near you. Talk to your child's cardiologist about linking you to other parents like yourself.

When I fall and skin my knee, Mommy and Daddy clean my boo-boo and give me a bandaid to wear until it feels better.

Baby has a boo-boo on baby's chest. Can you see the bandage?

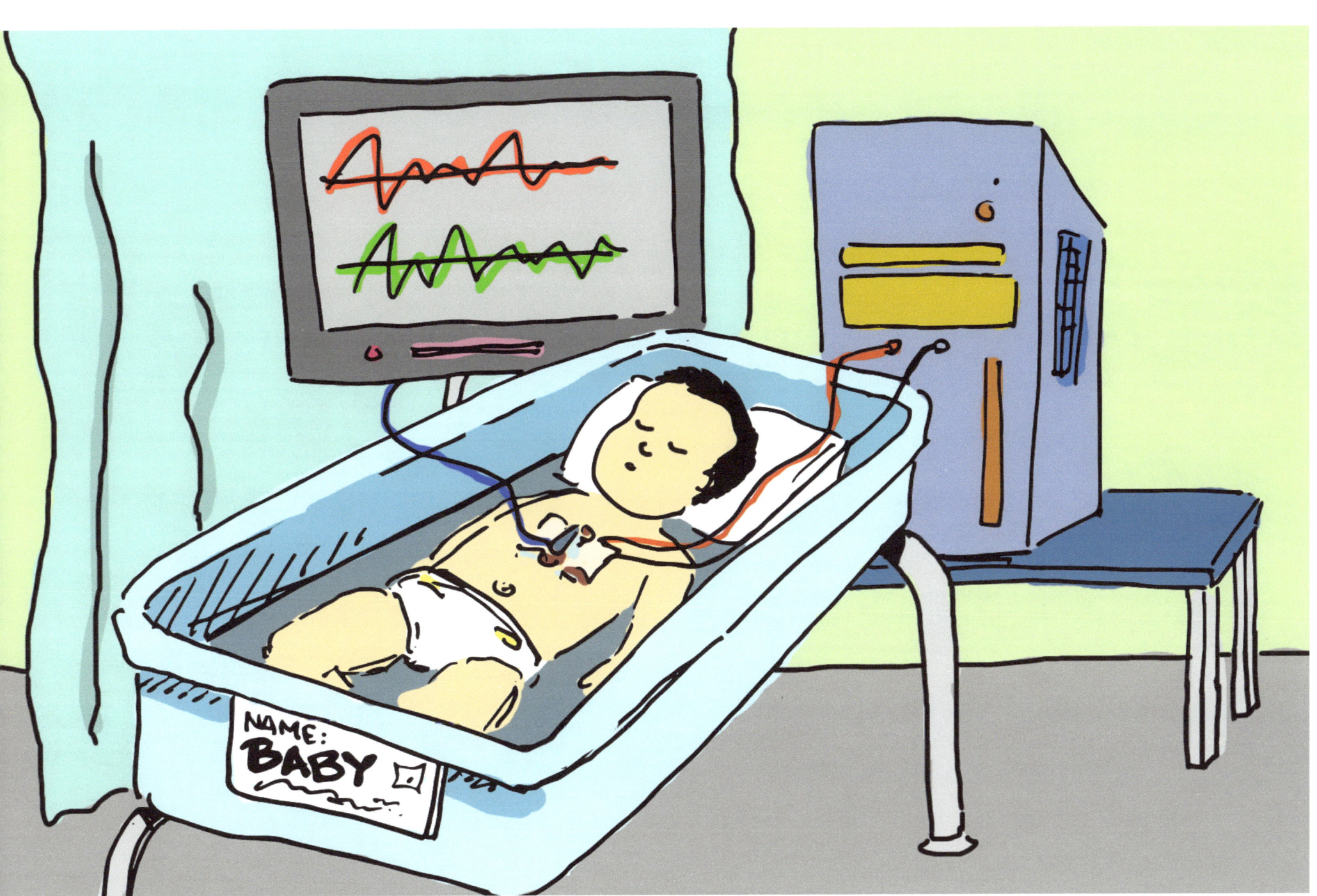

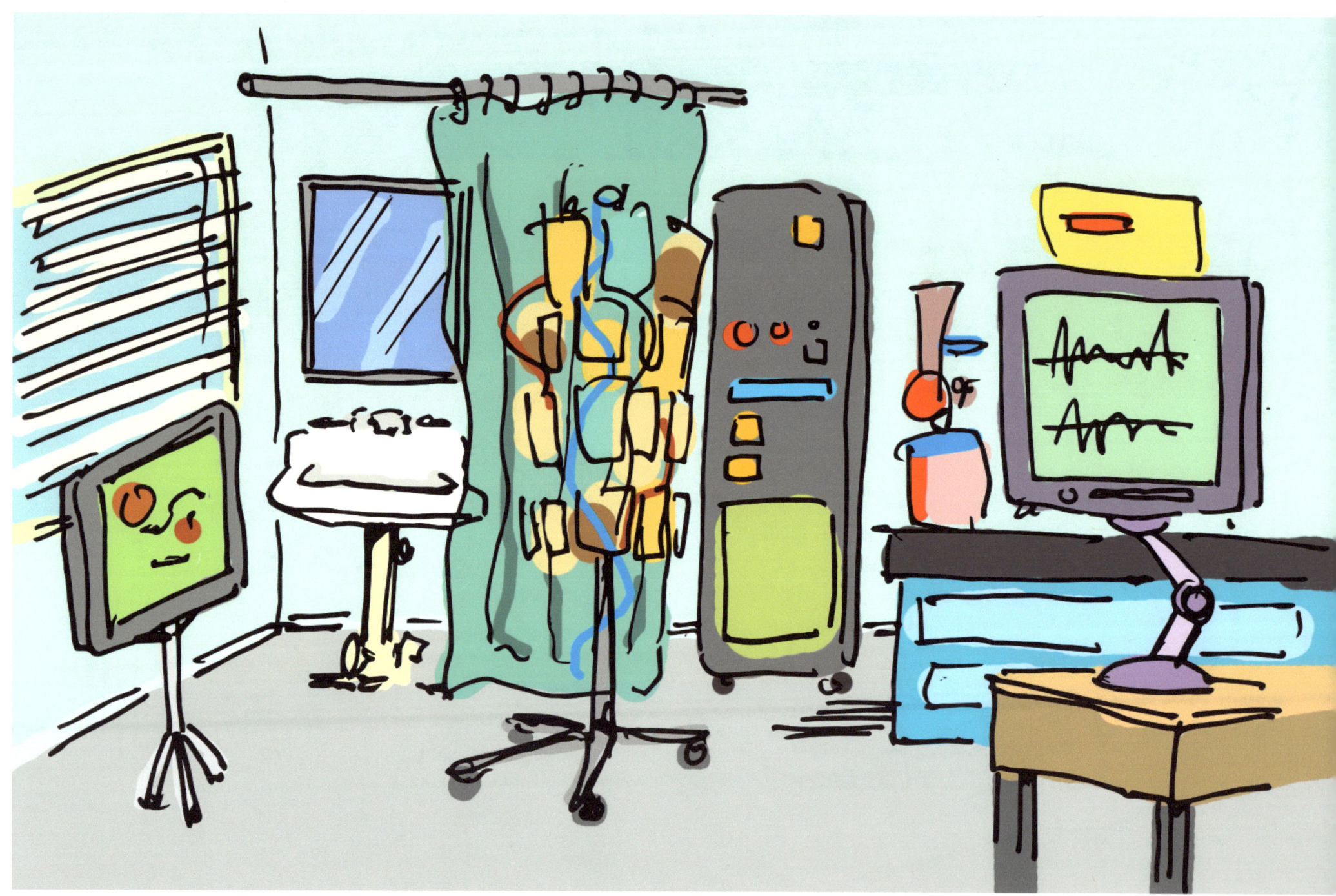

There are lots of machines in Baby's room. They have lights and make all kinds of noises. They help the doctors and nurses know how Baby is feeling.

Baby has lots of wires, too. Medicines go through the wires to help Baby get better.

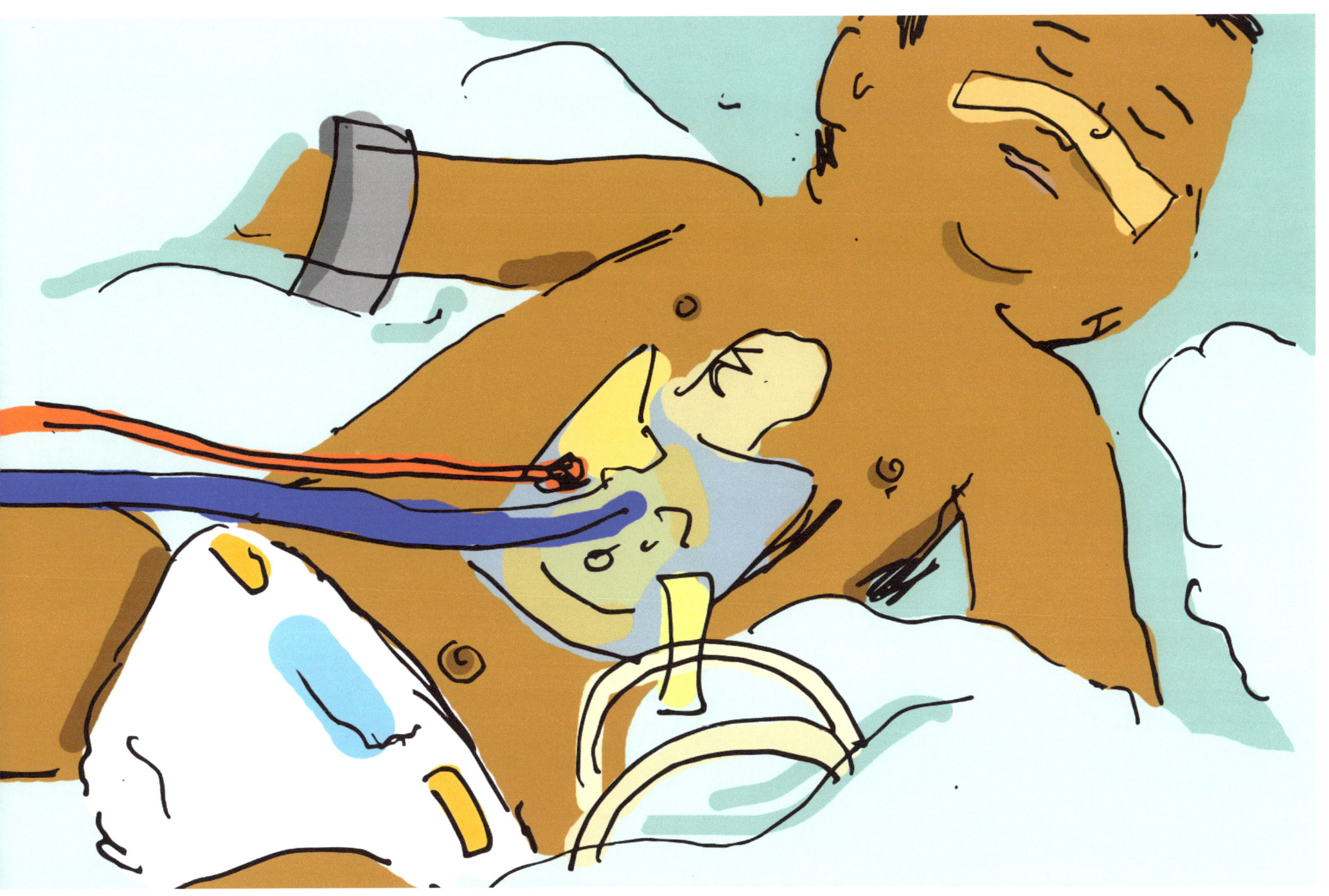

I am so excited I can visit Baby in the hospital with Mommy and Daddy!

I always wash my hands before seeing Baby.

I can kiss Baby on the top of the head. I can touch Baby on the feet.

I can bring pictures I draw at home to cheer Baby up.

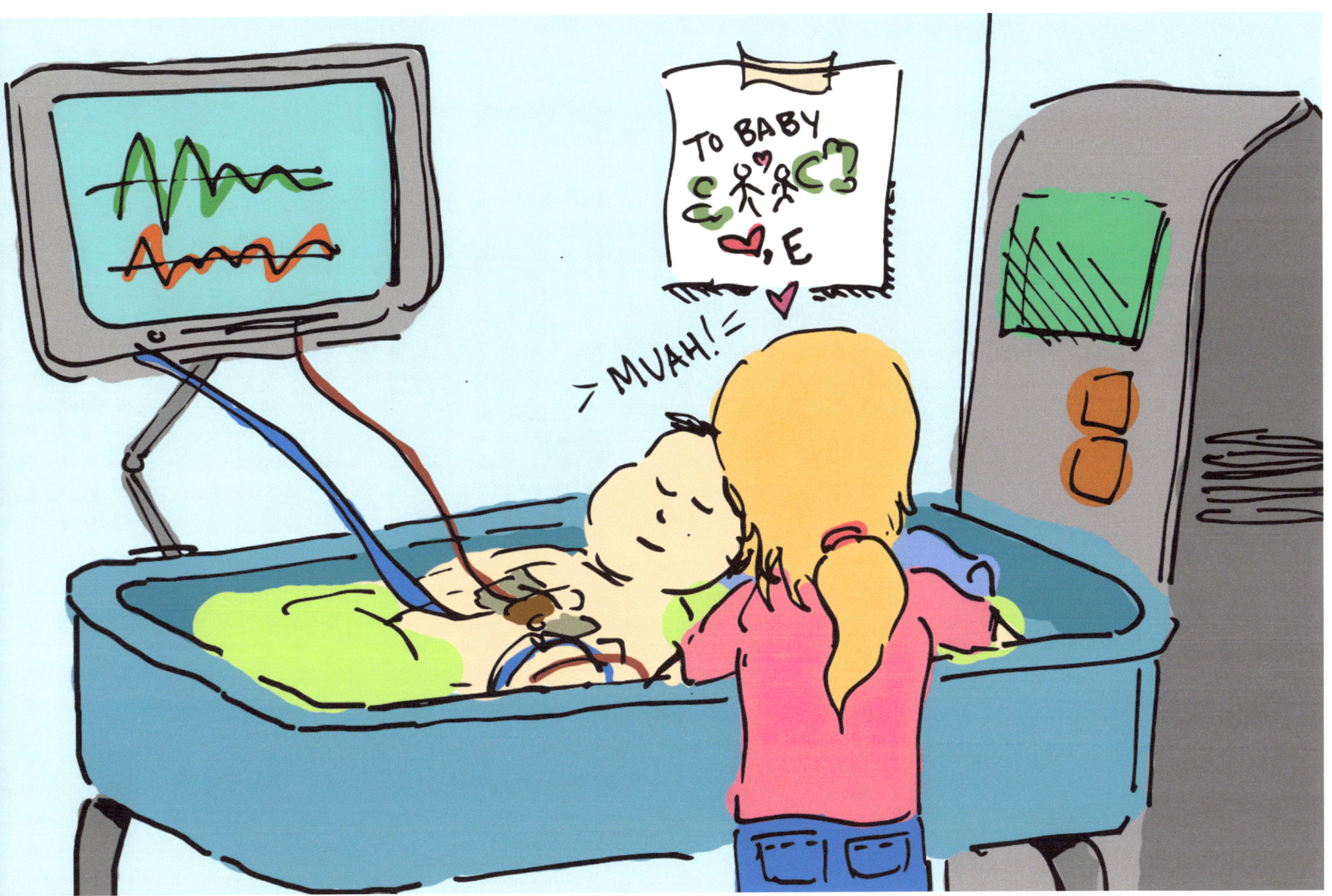

Sometimes, Mommy and Daddy go to the hospital without me. When they are away I stay with family and friends.

I miss Mommy and Daddy, but I know they will always come home.

There is always someone there to hold and love Baby, even when I'm at home with Mommy and Daddy.

A nurse watches over Baby every day and night.

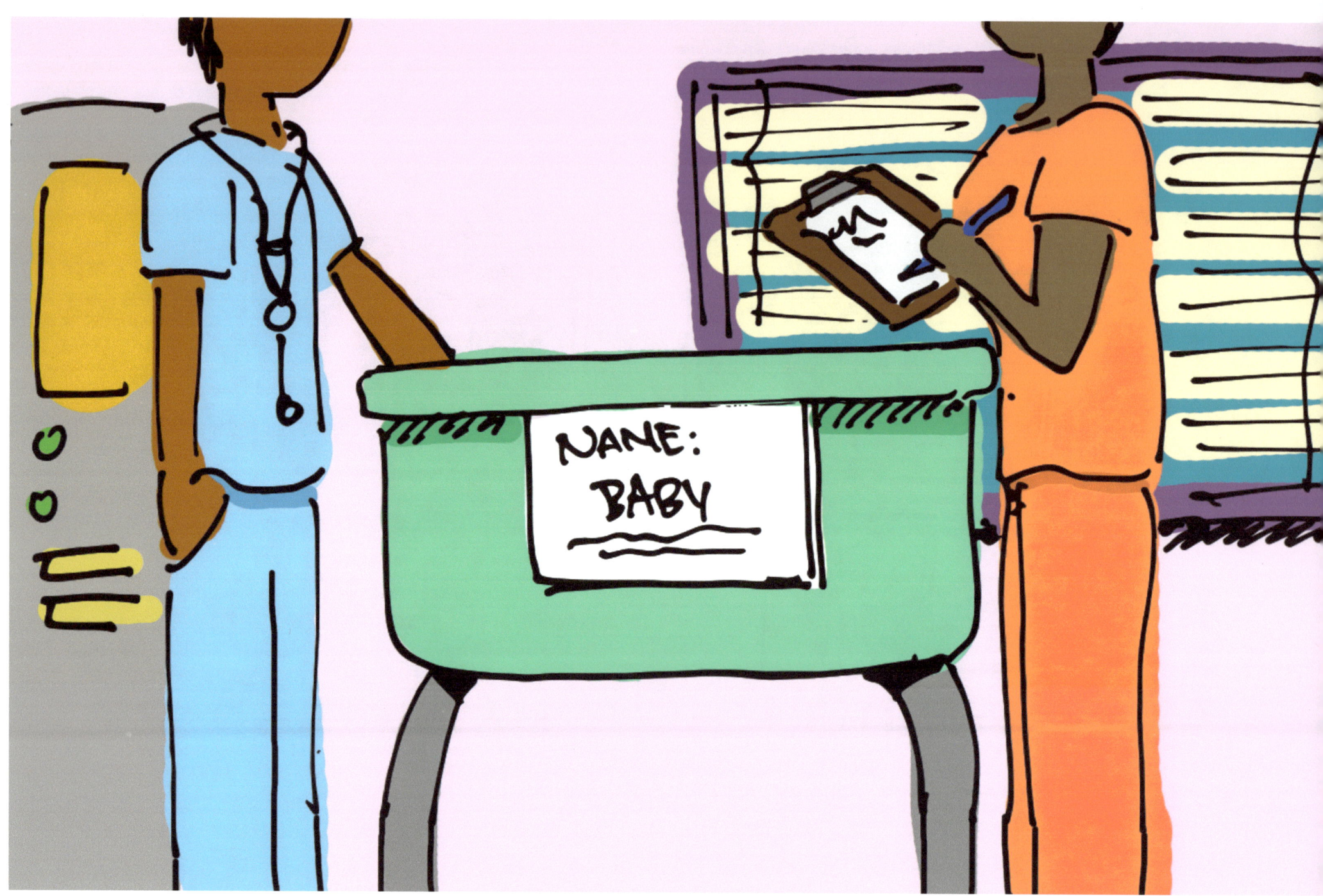

Baby lives at the hospital until the doctors say it is ok to go home. It can take a long time for Baby to feel better. I feel sad because I miss Baby.

I love Baby and will be so happy when Baby comes home to live with me.

Come home soon, Baby!

The Authors

Jenna Pratt is a working Heart Mom with a passion for CHD awareness and advocacy following the birth of her son who was diagnosed with Hypoplastic Left Heart Syndrome (HLHS) and who died unexpectedly of heart-related complications in September 2020. She holds a BA in Literature from North Georgia University. In her spare time, she enjoys photography, painting, and reading great science fiction.

Jenna, her husband, and two daughters live in Durham, North Carolina. You can follow their story on her blog: https://heartwarriorparenting.blogspot.com/

Dana Langston, PsyD., is a Licensed Psychologist who feels honored to work with children, adolescents, and adults in Raleigh, NC. She loves being mama to her two sons, daughter, and Old English Sheepdog. In her free time, Dana and her husband like binge watching funny shows on Netflix!

Maggie French is a freelance illustrator and painter living in Savannah, GA. As an illustrator, Maggie does work for a variety of small businesses. Maggie received her BFA in Studio Art from UNC-Chapel Hill. In her free time, Maggie enjoys drawing, cooking, and going on kayak adventures in the marsh around Savannah with her husband, Hansen. To check out more of her work, visit www.maggiebfrench.com

www.ingramcontent.com/pod-product-compliance
Lightning Source LLC
Chambersburg PA
CBHW041324290426

44108CB00005B/126